Rock Creek Blues

Rock Creek Blues

COTEAU
BOOKS

Edited by Robert Currie
Cover photograph by James R. Page
Design and typesetting by Susan Buck
Printed and bound in Canada by Impremerie Gauvin

Library and Archives Canada Cataloguing in Publication

Poirier, Thelma
    Rock Creek blues / Thelma Poirier.

Poems.
ISBN 978-1-55050-455-2

    I. Title.

PS8581.O233R62 2011   C811'.54   C2010-907068-2

10 9 8 7 6 5 4 3 2 1

COTEAU
BOOKS

2517 Victoria Avenue
Regina, Saskatchewan
Canada   S4P 0T2
www.coteaubooks.com

Available in Canada from:
Publishers Group Canada
2440 Viking Way
Richmond, British Columbia
Canada   V6V 1N2

Coteau Books gratefully acknowledges the financial support of its publishing program by: the Saskatchewan Arts Board, the Canada Council for the Arts, the Government of Canada through the Canada Book Fund, the Government of Saskatchewan through the Creative Economy Entrepreneurial Fund and the City of Regina Arts Commission.

for family and friends

Table of Contents

the January file

call this place home

with wind and bone

something old

what is it –
a handful of earth pressed against her face
clay from the banks of Rock Creek, sand and ash
she breathes, breathes
as though earth is air
recognizes
      this place
      these red buttes   so old
and her words scatter the way flakes scatter in a quarry
      in the beginning was the word
and the word was already old

badlands

we want to take visitors to see grass
it is not grass they want to see
it is badlands
dry gulches and adobe hills
streaks of colour grey on rose
layers of concealed fossils
and on the surface
varves along an ancient shore
clumps of primrose, sage
scattered cacti

visitors are led by postcards
have heard stories of badlands
great adventures, rustlers, outlaws
are not content with subtleties of grass
prefer badlands
            a dry crotch in a sea of grass

triceratops

sure, we know the place
where paleontologists from winnipeg/toronto
uncovered fossils
how they hauled them out by the wagonload
we saw the white deposit
the smudge on the face of a grey adobe

we know how others came
from other distant places, texas/arkansas
removed the skeleton of triceratops
left a gaping hole
in the side of a hill

we followed Sternberg from dig to dig
became amateur paleontologists
casually picking up stray bones
storing them in attics or in cellars
the same fossils are the missing pieces in the puzzles
others try to solve

we cannot put them back
back in the places where we found them
we left no markers

the steamy breath of triceratops
hisses down our necks

bones. 1

the way it is with bones
the animals I loved
I bury them one year
and the next
they begin to inch
their way to the surface
skulls first
sockets and nostrils bare to the wind
skulls lying on mounds
projecting above the horizon
hollow chambers
I no longer recognize
chambers where prairie winds twist
sometimes change direction

bones.2

when I lugged
the bull's skull
seven miles up Rock Creek
it was not because
I thought the skull would speak
or even that I might listen
but because it was there
braced against the bank
shimmering beneath the water
staring at me
through a watery lens

and when I brought it home
        the skull, full of iron oxide
it was not because
it was more beautiful than any living thing
it was my legacy

by the time I was home I was inside
        staring out

bones.3

walking with cougars
wandering amongst sandstone
          cougars the colour of sandstone
my eyes drift beyond my bones
discover other landscapes
horizons that are not really horizons
only uncertainties
identities and cavities so similar
I can no longer discern the cougars
snarling in the stone
the sand glinting in their eyes
the mirage between us
unmeasured

the last scout

there, at the headwaters, he
joins the great nightwatcher on his rounds
winds among the aspen bluffs
curves past a patch of chokecherries
circles the hills, round and round to the summit
the high place where he touches stars
brushes the face of the nightwatcher

below, the lazy eyes of an owl peer through the aspen
a sly coyote sniffs the willows
a mallard, one eye tucked beneath her wing,
and a single frog wait

in these same hills are stones
concentric circles leading from one ridge to another
a chain of endless generations, once a large assembly
where sky meets earth
and lights tower above an ebony horizon

long before this vigil
another walked with the nightwatcher
carried a shield
a bow

who will watch these hills when the scout is gone?
                    the owl
who will walk in his steps?
                    the coyote

a vesper sparrow

the fence is just a fence
until the skeleton of a bird
dangles from a barb
perhaps it is a sparrow, a vesper sparrow
there is no way to name it now
not having studied the anatomy of birds
small differences in clavicles and wings

it hangs by the toes
mid-song it must have lost its balance
turned the clouds upside down
    or
        it was hung by the butcher bird

the fence proclaims the harmony
       notes of one last song
as bone sings with wind and wire
wire sings with wind and bone

high noon

five years
a memory transcends
reality
a moment in a wash of grey shale
    wings of crimson, ivory, ebony
lift
    and tremble over a pale umbrella plant
a memory not needing a name

five years later someone names the image
names the elusive butterfly
       apodemia mormo langei
tells me the metalmark is an endangered species

the Latin nomenclature soon forgotten
the afterimage remains

wolf willow, wolf berry

prairie wolves (I am not
writing about coyotes)
prairie wolves love wolf willow

watch the wolves
they are invisible
their shadows mark the spaces
where gray bodies
once wavered
amongst the wolf berry
wolf willow

prairie wolves
love moonlit nights
listen,
the song of the wolves trembles between the leaves
of wolf willow and wolf berry

prairie wolves
leave tracks without a trace
a scent lingering in wolf berry, wolf willow

coyote.1

out of the horizon
two coyote shapes emerge
                    grinning
biting following
each other in circles

only one coyote felt the circle
begin within her body
called the other to her tracks
now grinning
neither cares where the circle began

~

some coyote pups are watchers on the hill
some are runners   relay running
chasing a doe through the buckbrush
prairie bound coyotes close in
doe leaps
        coyotes slit her flank

blood leads them
                snarling
piecemeal they kill

some coyote pups are watchers on the hill

coyote.2

as memory becomes hunger
coyote sniffs a trail

no tracks, no wind, no scent
only the snow

the long dark of a cold December
each day like the day before

something is promised beyond the horizon
something essential

morning expels coyote from the hills
she runs the flats

soon the baited horse is ripped
from jaw to flank

coyote creeps into a den to sleep
her jaws tighten

her throat shrinks and death rumbles
on the other side of her dream

coyote.3

city coyote, country coyote

slip along the alleys
slip along the streets
scavengers patrol inner city nights
shadows prowl beneath fluorescent lights

cast a moonlight shadow
cast a moonlight howl
a melancholy concert a solitary will
no echo from the darkness no answer from the hill

~

coyote pup   curled into a muff
sleeps in a furrier's window
black lips   half pout   half grin
ears like penny purses half open
even with glass eyes
coyote pup watches us pass by

the last peregrine

first primeval, now cosmopolitan
you leave the barren cliff
the mountain mist
nest on skyscrapers

you acknowledge man
the structures created by man
balance eggs on concrete ledges
high above the walks
and windowsills where men and pigeons
shuffle summer mornings

some say you will soon be extinct
glass towers are a stop along the way

your final death will leave a hole
the size of a fist in the heart of man
a hole large enough for other birds
to fly through

where you fly
other birds will follow

traplines.1

someone shifts the animals
one by one to the city
the usual route
from hunger to trap
to padded hanger
animals no longer slide
between the trees
they exist in the open
folly of a coat

oh, the silken mink
trembling as I stroke
slip inside the fur
of the wild mink, wanting

I would be double woman
beautiful mink

~

the sudden snare
rabbit's last breath
flesh and fur
before the trapper arrives, mink
a dark shadow in the black pine
writes a scarlet signature on a white pelt

traplines.2

a wolverine springs a trap
before it takes the bait

a fox frees itself
chews
through its own leg

I am neither
wolverine nor fox

I am stunned
by my image in their eyes
the blue pain

park land

as a rancher moves out
prey and predators move in
the land claims its own

a pair of elk
are joined by three more
seventeen make a herd

last week a cougar was spotted
stalking two mares and a colt
on the banks of Rock Creek

in the far corner
of the west pasture
a prairie wolf enlarges a den

a wolverine
emerges from the shadows
black shadows of a poplar grove

ranch land becoming a park

wilderness begins with a *w*

I am the one
with flesh   with bone
born with a page between
me and the light the wind

I share a wilderness
chop down some trees
plant some others
turn a lot of stones
someone will turn again
I am always trading
a bear for a beaver
one wilderness for the next

I want to touch the wind
touch the things the wind touches
earth and wings and space
I want to tell what comes after

I am the one
crippled by the page
the one-eyed trapper

New Orleans, Saskatchewan

1.

One morning I sit in a patch of sunshine on the kitchen
floor. I am playing with Topsy-Turvy, flipping her skirt back
and forth, blue print, red gingham. Yellow hair, black hair.
White face, brown face. Mama isn't looking when I throw her
in the flour bin.

2.

On Rock Creek Mama makes bread pudding once a week.
She mixes the eggs and milk, cinnamon, nutmeg, raisins,
breaks the dry bread in chunks and stirs them into the pudding
pan. She stokes the fire, adds sticks of willow, pokes the pan of
bread pudding in the oven.

Mama serves the bread pudding in hobnail saucers. The
raisins stare at me from inside the chunks of pudding. When
no one is looking, I pick the raisins out and hide them under
the edge of my plate where they can't see me.

3.

Mama knows what she wants. She wants to climb on
board a riverboat at the headwaters of Rock Creek while the
water is high, float down to the Milk River, to the Missouri,
past the patches of wild plums on the riverbanks in Dakota,

past St. Louis and down the Mississippi, past the plantations to New Orleans.

The water is never high enough in Rock Creek and Mama is busy baking bread, canning berries and raising babies.

4.

Summer evenings when the scent of lilacs drifts through the veranda into the living room, Mama plays the blues on a Kimball piano – *Old Man River*, and *Across the Wide Missouri*, *Won't You Come Home, Bill Bailey?*, *Frankie and Johnny*. Hey, you say, that's not the blues. Well, it is blues when Mama plays it. It is water music as one note slides into the next, as Mama drifts downstream, finally arrives in New Orleans.

The scent of lilacs lingers.

5.

Mama is making a baby quilt for a granddaughter. She embroiders ducks and kittens, lambs and a pony on blocks cut from flour sacks.

The baby is LaVaun.

6.

LaVaun is three years old. She wins a pony in the Kiwanis raffle in Moose Jaw. A photographer takes her picture sitting in a saddle on the pony. The picture is printed in the *Moose Jaw Times Herald*. She can not keep the pony, her parents live in the city.

7.

Fats Domino is coming. Not to Rock Creek, to Calgary, to the Corral. Charlene and I are going. We line up at the box office, wait two hours in a March rain, lean against the side of the Corral, Charlene is singing *My Blue Heaven*.

Two weeks later we return to the Corral, stand in line again. At last we're inside. It's so crowded on the main floor, we can't see our shoes. The back-up act comes on, plays *Green Door* and *Wake Up Little Susie* and *Be Bop a Lula*. A man in a black suit comes out on stage, the crowd presses forward. The man in the black suit announces that the show has been cancelled. We start to chant,

We want Fats. We want Fats.

The back-up plays *My Blue Heaven* and a riot breaks out in the Corral. Shoes, purses, lipstick , mirrors and combs scatter across the stage. Next to us, four or five zoot-suiters rattle their chains.

8.

Far from home we have assembly at Mount Royal College. After announcements by Dean Collett, there is always some sort of feature - maybe one of the students from the conservatory singing - a contralto or a mezzo soprano, maybe a guest speaker.

Jackie Robinson comes in November. It is the year after the Dodgers win the World Series. All the while I am listening to him my mind is jumping back and forth - from Jackie to Topsy-Turvy.

9.

Assembly at Mount Royal again. It is raining, too wet to walk down by the river, the river runs deeper than Rock Creek. Another soprano, another contralto. Not this time, this time it is Eric. Eric wears blue suede shoes, a pale yellow V-neck, cashmere, sleeves pushed up. His hair is duck-tailed in the back, tousled over his eyes in front. In his hand he carries a saxophone.

I don't know what Eric is supposed to play, but that day he plays the blues. He lets the kettle steam and boil, he moves it from the back of the stove and sets it down on the fire. He empties the reservoir.

Ever after I am always yearning for something just beyond my grasp.

10.

Regina to Minneapolis. The ground is white with snow. Farms sit like spots on dice, snake eyes and box cars, Little Richard and sevens. Seven, come eleven.

Minneapolis to Lusianne. There, off to my right, there's the Mississippi. My first glimpse and I swallow, swallow to keep the water down. Mama's river.

Mama, how you doing, all scrunched up in my pocket?

11.

I read the sign on LaVaun's door.

Please telephone in advance

please telephone

please…

What's your number, LaVaun?

Last year there were 2,474 new cases of AIDS in New Orleans where LaVaun lives. Lives inside her bones.

What's your case number, LaVaun?

12.

LaVaun is making a grandmother's quilt for her daughter.

She's paddling upstream as the names come tumbling down –

Bruiette, Chausee, Arnold, Rideau, Grandon, Monroe

and somewhere a Wyandot, a girl without a name

I hold one side of the quilt, LaVaun holds the other.

She hums as she quilts:

Make a joyful noise unto the Lord.

Make a joyful noise.

This is her first quilt. It may be her last.

13.

On her last birthday LaVaun buys an Arabian pony. Aletia Missy Lee. Missy Lee. She is such a spoiled pony, she was raised in a house, expects her carrots to be ground, her apples to be quartered. At the stable I put my arms around Missy Lee, bury my sorrow in her mane. Pretty pony. We are both standing in the same swamp.

14.

I stand on the levee in New Orleans.

New Orleans.

Listen, honey, we don't say Orleens, it's New Orlens.

Listen, honey.

I listen and I hear voices, floating down river, great grumbling barges, liners – smooth as silk, ships plying muddy water, little tugs and a dredge going down deep, coming up muddy. This is the Mississippi.

The river churns and roils beyond the barriere. There's so much music in that cafe au lait, one note trembling beside the next, I can't hold it in my cup. The spoon rattles.

15.

At the Lusianne Cajun Cookin' School I learn to make bread pudding. Raisin pudding with whiskey sauce. Pineapple pudding with pina colada. Peach pudding with butterscotch schnapps. Blueberry pudding with grenadier.

And never, ever beat the eggs.

16.

I eat bread pudding at Pere Antoine's. I tell the waiter it is good bread pudding. *Oh yes,* he says, *but not as good as my mama makes.*

I eat bread pudding at Michaud's. It is better than the bread pudding at Pere Antoine's. I tell the waiter it is good bread pudding. *Oh yes,* he says, *but not as good as my mama makes.*

I eat bread pudding at Mr. B's. It is better than the pudding at Michaud's. *Oh yes,* the waiter says, *but*

not as good as

my mama makes.

17.

I ride the Creole Queen, Mississippi water

Somewhere Johnny Horton sings *The Battle of New Orleans*

I ride Esplanade and Chartres, Royale and Decatur

this is a decadent life

It's a *Train They Call the City of New Orleans*

and I can't find the station, can't get off.

18.

Ski Jam.

I ask a New Orleans jazz band to play Ski Jam
and the man on the saxophone says to me,

*Lady, you in the wrong place. This ain't no Aspen, Colarada,
ain't no snow here. This here New Orlens, the real blues.*

And the man on the saxophone begins to play
Bill Bailey, Won't You Please Come Home?

And when the man says *Take it away*

the ghost of Mama slips onto the piano bench,
starts to play.

19.

This is WKCT-TV, New Orleans and now for the weather:

*The coldest city in North America last night was Regina,
Saskatchewan. Comin' in at minus thirty-eight. The big chill is
movin' south. The magnolia buds are turning brown. We got
weather.*

20.

We make groceries. Melinde's Hot Sauce, Cajun Power,
Zatarain's File, Ellis Stansel's rice...

We'll have jambalaya, crawfish pie and file gumbo

mix the spice, stir it twice, spicy nice

for tonight we're gonna squeeze our acadia mia

we'll be warm in New Orleans, Saskatchewan

son of a gun we'll have big fun on
Rock Creek Bayou

21.

Mama made pancakes on Shrove Tuesday. She went to the
grocery store and bought a package of Aunt Jemima's pancake
mix. She mixed the batter, greased the griddle and cooked
those pancakes as fast as we could eat them.

That was Mardi Gras on Rock Creek.

22.

Laura Plantation.

I stand on the back veranda of the main villa, look across
the yard, past the kitchen, past the horse stable, past the
blacksmith shop to the slave cabins. A mist hangs in the air
between the cabins.

Topsy-Turvy, where you at?   Waiting.

23.

Laura Plantation.

Back in time that's where Alcee Fortier collected the stories of Compair Lapin, the most famous rabbit in the universe, and Piti Bondhomme Godron, the tar baby. Br'er Rabbit, now I know where you come from.

The wine cellar is empty. So is the library. No one sits at the dining room table. No one is fanning the guests. No one is serving dinner from the kitchen. The kitchen is a gift shop. Topsy-Turvy sits on a shelf beside Bondhomme Godron.

24.

Laura,

You were in Lusianne long before I was born,

I knew you then

you spoke French on your plantation

English waited outside on the step

Laura with your forty slaves, your four hundred acres, your private cemetery

Laura, are you listening?

25.

On Bourbon Street an old man and a young man reach back, way back, bring up a harmonica and a banjo. They begin to play, play some of those low-down dirty blues. A crowd gathers. Dollars float into the banjo case. The old man grins, his single tooth, pink gums shine in the morning light. The old man and the young man josh back and forth.

In the middle of a song the young man pauses – shouts to a hustler passing by

You son-a-bitch, you ain't spoilin' my party this mo'nin'.

The old man says

Never pay him no mind, man. We here to make music.

And the old man lifts the harmonica to his lips and plays some notes so blue, they're the colour of indigo.

26.

We eat at Rita's. The maitre d' sits us in the center aisle with the rest of the white folks. On either side black men and women lean against the walls, drink wine and watch us eat. I see the old man who played the harmonica, and a young girl with pigtails laughing beneath a poster that says Bo Diddley is coming to town next week. We eat our oyster po'boys and our chocolate suicide.

27.

One more trip across the Mississip, one more trip on the ferry from Canal Street to old Algiers, to the part of town where LaVaun lives. Old Algiers, that's where the slaves were stalled before they went to market.

One time or another we're all slaves, only we don't know it yet. Not yet. Not until we're free. Ain't that right, Laura?

28.

In the backyard among the palmettos, the magnolias and the yams there is a concrete angel. Her wings are raised slightly. She hovers over the garden. I ask LaVaun about the angel.

She says, *Angel? My angel?*

29.

Down the street from LaVaun's house, an ancient oak, three, four, five hundred years old, shades the sidewalk, its roots spread over the lawn like gnarled writing. I am as old as the oak.

On the levee, I lean into the wind, breathe Mississippi air, a cool breeze blowing in from the river. I am as old as the river.

And on the riverwalk someone plays a saxophone, plays a song that hasn't been written. Not yet.

30.

Regina. Minus forty-one.

Like a trombone reaching for that last note. We're in a
slide.

31.

Home from New Orleans, back on Rock Creek.

Mama, where you at?

Where you learn to play the blues? Was it pickin'

berries on the banks of the Missouri, watchin'

riverboats float downstream?

Mama, are you still in my pocket?

fence lines

a measure of fence

the first day
an eye is threaded
on the wire

it bumps along

blind
to all
but the barbs

~

the fields of barley
the cows
the pastures
disappear

the eye is on the fence

long
thin
wire

~

the eye looks
down the wire
post melds into post

fence lines
become
line fences

~

a mile of fence
        bar
                    post
                            mallet
        wire
                    staple
                            hammer
dreams stapled
to diamond willow

~

when the wire breaks
the strands recoil
barbs jiggle

the eye rolls
across the prairie

~

a sideways glance:
        prairie chickens
deep in sage
        drum and dance
in circular admiration

advance
retreat
flaunt their feathers
incessantly
     taunting
prairie chickens

~

the eye returns
to the wire

~

jaws of red
jaws of yellow
teeth of red and yellow

wire stretchers
clamped on wire
wire song
repairing wire

~

a thistle
convolutes
madly
     forward
and reverse

tenuous
a shadow dancing
in a February storm

~

after snow
winter
      strands
            of stars
                  on the fence

summer
      lightning skips
along the top wire

the eye comes and goes

~

a fence is never finished

wild flowers

moving to the prairie, there are things you should know
neighbors will forget to tell you

and you can not read them in the Farmer's Almanac
they are not printed on paper

the lure of wild flowers
small addictions in petal and stamen

where the larkspur grows,
how to recognize the plant before it blossoms

the purple poison; how a cow died
and three heifers aborted their calves

because no one was watching for larkspur, and
another year it was a filly

chomping on locoweed; and what of nightshade
it dealt a double death, a team of horses

wild flowers,
the colours of death

December morning

I breathe on a frosted window
melt a peephole
watch as my father rides
out of a blizzard
      his horse frosted, too

watch as he jingles past a red shed
      past a clutch of willow
back into the blizzard

a page from my mother's writing tablet
      becomes white flakes on white vellum

      see, see my picture
      see my father

no one else can see him
inside the blizzard
riding through the page
toward me

none of this may be the way it happened
it is the way I remember

old blue

years, my father's guitar
stood in the space between the piano
and the wall

I remember once
my father played guitar
        a lonely New Year's Eve
ranch hands saddled up, gone off to town

I listened to him play
a wistful, tantalizing tune
        of border towns, cantinas
places he had never been
                blue Spanish eyes
        a hesitant melody
he played for girls he never met
and maybe old regret

he played the same song twice
for cowboys he once knew
boys that brandished foolish guns
nighthawks that never saw the sun
wranglers and those who rode the drag
played for cooks and *tin cans by the fire*
for coyotes on the hill
        for dusty trails and longhorns
and he played for saddle tramps

on New Year's Eve
my father played guitar

*Italics represent lines from a poem titled *Rekindling Campfires*
written by the author's great-grandfather.

Hellfire Creek

that's where the LA calves were branded
when I was a child

my father
one or two of my brothers
a hired man
rode in from the north,
others came from the camp
circled, came in from the west
bunched the cattle as they came
herded them into the corral

branding day
I hung on the top rail
lined up empty vaccine bottles
I was too little to help
just big enough to get in the pictures

the last LA cattle
were branded in the same corrals
a ritual re-enacted
this time I sat on the top rail
watched older brothers, sisters take their turn
waited, knowing my turn would come too soon

I clenched the LA irons
pressed the irons against the calf's hide
my eyes blurred, the sting of smoke
all that was lost
my father's knife in one hand
the calf's sack in the other

one swipe of the blade
I held testicles,
pulled each one down
scraped the cords
the same way I saw my father do it

it was my turn

line fences

one quarrel too many
    a splintered post
    staples popping
    barbed wire tangled
    cows straying back and forth
    bulls following
    or maybe it was a gate left open
one angry word echoing another
they know other words
        forgive, forget
let those words fester between the teeth and the lower lip
someone suggests they
        write their differences in the snow
        let the sun settle them in the spring

    they wait for high water

another rancher's prayer

out here on the ranch
let us be thankful
for blessings town folk have never known
for stillborn calves
because the mama's didn't die
for colts
and mares with milk enough for one more day
for stackyards half full of moldy hay
for dogs too old to stir
and cats with kittens that do not match
for gates that haven't fallen down
and fence posts that stand up on their own
for fencing pliers we have lost and found
and lucky gloves, the same
for reins that do not snap
for leather worn thin, not worn out
for wood that will burn better in a year
for creeks that never will go dry
for droughts that save us from a flood
and floods that only wash a little soil away
for grass we never have to mow
for winds that blow the snow away
and turn around and blow it back again another day
for Stanfield's woolen underwear
and four ply socks
for too much work to do today
and thanks for giving us this "try"
for hitchin' up our wagons when we're down
and most of all
for places that are far from town

not a toy horse

Memory inadvertently allows an old horse
(old she supposes because it is dead)

to enter the kitchen; she is slicing ripe tomatoes
at the time, and for that reason maintains

she is unaccountable for its presence,
as is the horse. It leans against her

the way dead horses do, surrounding itself
with dim lights, straw harness

hanging from the rafters. The horse is stuffed
stuffed as though it were a bag of loose oats

and toothless, too. Better than a toy horse,
a runaway galloping through the willows

the ride ends in this kitchen. Her disbelief gleams
in its glass eyes, the colour of tomatoes.

~

The second time she saw the horse, saddled and
tied to a hitching post inside a bar

she was still not a believer, though someone
told her, or she read that years ago

Roy stuffed Trigger; but this old paint
moon blind and moth eaten

makes no pretensions. He was nobody's
rope horse, nobody's racing pride

just a school pony, now tied in a bar
for no apparent reason, yet

he leads into her dreams. Morning
finds him tied to her bedpost.

this poem .

begins in darkness
     moonless winter night

resident owls are hunched
beneath their wings
     the night, too dark

along the lane
not a tinkle as frost
     tightens barbed wire

standing in snow
an old horse
     hoofs, fetlocks, knees
wobble in a circle of coyotes
a strident chorus declares
the omnipotence of winter

this poem ends in silence

family fences

a family fixes fences
moves from post to post
mending

> I walk ahead, lean into diamond willow
> posts slowly rotting
> pull staples out, undo wire
>
> our son follows
> his eye on the line
> the next horizon
> he sets new posts in place
>
> his child runs back and forth
> carries staples
> learns the place where the sagehen nests
> where the coyote makes its den and which
> cry is the ferruginous hawk
> which, the prairie falcon
> learns our names for flowers
> shooting stars and buffalo beans
> absorbs the scent of wolf willow
>
> and you, coming behind
> you staple old wire to new posts

each spring this is the way
a family fences

the Rock Creek waltz

in what season of joy she lingered at the piano

      emerald shadows
            reflected in summer sun
      green, lilting through moss and fern
      redolence beneath black poplar

      each autumn
      a measure of water pressing against willow
      willow leaves drifting downstream
      away from her

      beneath the ice
      the quietness of water
            and all hell ready to break loose
      high water, there the first joy of spring

a waltz
      tumbling from the headwaters

Louise

a heifer heaves
turns her body inside out
calf and calfbed steaming in the yellow straw

a young woman knots the calf bed
tight around her fist
leans into the heifer's hip
pushes, shoves the knot inside
pulls her arm out of darkness

the calf bed follows
iridescent in the pale light

she begins again

hours later, wet and weak
she goes to the house for the gun

memory: a blurred image
the heifer's eye

regulations

say she can not use the gun
again, can not shoot the coyote
sneaking into the yard
to snatch the kittens on her porch
maybe grab her daughter's arm
as she stacks wooden blocks on the patio

she runs for the gun
presses it into her shoulder
closes her eyes
and shoots

coyote flops on the front grass
its tongue lolling
its eyes so small
she must squint
to see if it is really dead

one for the sheep

I met a woman in Elko
should have known she raised sheep
had more than a hundred ewes to lamb next month

there were enough signs –
her joints, knick-a-knack
as she walked across the platform

her bleary eyes
the colour of California sage
her woolly hair

the way she ate lamb at Biloxi's
almost reluctantly – tiny bites

and the way she bleated out her poems
soft as evening air
I should have known she raised sheep

a thousand miles apart
we write letters

she tells me about the ewes
bagged out and lambing
lambs, one after another stillborn
without reason

darkness filled with poetry
her sheep camp silent

this one's for Amanda

beyond the canola fields, a village
dusty shoes walk down dusty lanes
intent upon the jail, the only space large enough
to frame a quilt
                    this one's for Amanda

men swallow the last of their steaming potato soup
return to patchwork of their own
stand on tractors
pondering what makes a woman
pull the blinds, leave the shade within a house
engage the buzz of black flies and the chatter of other women
what drives a woman to cut bolts of cloth
precisely in geometric pieces
and stitch them back together again

chokecherries

this moment in the berry patch
our arms bending the same branch down
your sleeve and mine
snagged on the same burr
I can hear your joy   your pain   purple berries
you drop them in your pail
filling it again
              again

at birth
I was not your sister
now I am

five songs for a quartet

1.

waiting
the night demands a gentle sound
snow
          rushing
the sound of white

                    hush
          the child turns
in the basket

she is never quite sure

          a ptarmigan unzips the night
          beneath the boughs

sorrow is the sound
stillborn

2.

she carries the child like a stone
afraid of the insensibility
the inevitability of life

the child, the birthstone
insists

and she is huge

a boulder weighs her down
          in the garden
          in the middle of the night
her bed is not a refuge
the stone demands its life

when the stone comes grinding its way out of the womb
twisting its blood-blotched body
flailing its limbs
deep in its throat
a pit breaks
and language attaches itself
begins crying
from the inside out

3.

already a grandmother
she should not bear another child
the present fetus,
　　　　regret

at the solstice
she listens as hunters talk
tell how a doe absorbs a fetus
slowly into its body during a hard winter

the sharp hoofs of a fawn protest
strike the walls of her womb
　　　this may be a hard winter

4.

      gone yesterday
here today
      snow interlocks
earth and sky
         white
as a communion dress

nothing so white has she seen
~

this waiting room is a white room
             a white light
        on a white bed
where you lie
your shadow is invisible
it is tucked beneath you
          white

5.

there are always angels
pulling duty
        (and overtime)
early morning he calls
fifteen angels
from the angel pool

in the ambulance
he is the only one
who can hear the sirens singing

after surgery
they hang around
the way angels do

he can smell them
the strong scent of angels
loitering

a pair of owls

three days
owl rides the bough
sways through the gentle storm

winds lift suspend the snow
above the yard drop the sky into the chimney

owl sits aloof
ignores snow
sparrows huddled in a bush below

owl stares
at the window where she waits
sometimes rotates his head
left to right   right to left
binocular eyes intent

by night she cheats
buries her face in his ruff
his great wings spread from wall to wall
flap silently

by day clouds filter the sun
light shines
through the brazen eyes of the owl

when she learns to fly
a platonic lover will not be enough

owl leaves the evergreen bough

after sunset
      before dark
she wants to fly with him
let her shadow skip with his
share a synchronized flight

sharp talons drag her through glass

window panes

when he dies
she imagines windows
where houses no longer exist

a clump of trees
birches bending
within a square of glass

a narrow window
defines the bulging belly
of a moose
it slumbers

a circular window
shrinks the sun

and the moon is a sliver
of broken glass

the house of blessings

she knows where she is going
that same place
she saw in their eyes
the moments after their births
before their gaze met hers
the moments when she knew they came
from the house of blessings

now, as slowly,
she carries her pain to that place
they line up outside her door
      gangly men in boys' clothing
      young women wanting answers
call her *mother*
      in small voices
they know she is tripping
lightly over the threshold
returning to the house of blessings

the January file

January, the first

the first game of the year
we play Rummoli
deal cards around a kitchen table
start out equal
each of us has fifty matchsticks
the cards are in control
some of us drift to television
other conversations
those who play the game are fierce
must win, form coalitions
bump shoulders, jostle, laugh
the game is flawed

~

I am part of the conversation
we talk as though the war is just over the big hill
grinding its way toward us, irreversible
a niece says it will be finished in a day
her uncle thinks it will last for months
maybe even years

conversations, and somewhere a prayer
sticks between the tongue and the lips

January, the fourth

for two weeks we try to move the cows home
they will not leave the creek bottom
are exposed to bitter weather
wind and temperature: the combined factors
minus forty, minus fifty
cows huddle in the brush
clods of snow stick to their hides
icicles on their lashes
their muzzles, beards of frost

we coax them from the brush
this day, they surrender
follow single file
the sounds, knuckles cracking
the hollow crunch of snow

you walk behind the cows
your toes cold as metal typewriter keys
I drive the truck, am warm inside the cab
I listen to the radio
talk of war
a Middle East advisor outlines precautions
soldiers must follow in the Arabian desert
lessons in survival

January, the sixth

morning comes bright as yellow straw
snowflakes melt on the hillside
slush is inevitable

before dark, wind bites at the jaw
snow pricks like pitchforks
ice prevails

weather report follows the news
the way war follows peace
two faces of January

January, the ninth

everyone is talking about young men
death in the desert
seven thousand hospital beds are reserved in London
additional security comes on duty at the airport in Regina
in the event of war I am not sure what special steps
I am supposed to take
it is hard to realize the desert exists
when I am feeding cows
the temperature is minus thirty degrees
the four-wheel drive will not start

January, the tenth

I watch too much television
I have cramps, can feel the rough edges of a walnut
travelling through me, a sense of worms
tunnelling, the nut empty inside
I tell myself to turn the television off
already it is too late,
I am waiting for a blackout

we move four yearling bulls from one pen to another
load them in a trailer
in low range the four-wheel drive can not climb the hill
it is icy and you back down to take another run
another and another; some days the truck
can not pull four bulls up a hill
there must be another way to do this

January, the twelfth

I am in a very small room
a cubbyhole
I ask myself what I am doing inside this television
it is only a twenty-four inch cabinet,
and why am I crawling into this bodysuit
slipping this gas mask over my head
rehearsing

January, the thirteenth

the situation today is deteriorating
every broadcast is an echo of the one before

instant replay as the deadline approaches
I am on standby, clutching my gut

this is the third time I have felt ill in as many days
each time it was different; the first time a billy goat

chewed its sour cud in my stomach, second was a headache
bronze camel bells clanging behind my eyes and presently

the grumblings of a great bear, thin and restless
turning over and over in the last hours of hibernation

Yes, I would say the situation is deteriorating
I am losing the first battle before the war begins

January, the fourteenth

across Canada there are old bomb shelters
tins of food inside them, forgotten, rusted
radio batteries, leaking

they say there is a shelter in town
beneath the ground where the station used to be
the site has been paved over

if anyone knows where the entrance is located
no one is telling, perhaps it is across the street
hidden behind a false wall in the abandoned store
what about the outhouse halfway down the block
or Mrs. Wilson's root cellar
is there a tunnel to the school, the Mayor's office
the pool hall?
is there an unlisted number?

January, the fifteenth

early morning all is white
the neighbours' farms, the trees that line their drives
our farm, the fences that separate us
even the shadows

the silence of the morning is the silence of white
sky and fog retreating into the hills
silence prevails
ominous

January, the fifteenth

late morning
I can not understand why I am baking bread
the breadbox is full

the yeast bubbles up like small battles
I dump it in a pan of warm water, add salt, sugar
flour, and I stir with a wooden spoon
stir crazy, the batter thickens, more flour
the punching begins
I don't know why I am punching the dough so hard
I don't know why I am punching

~

we are contained in a January cold spell
we think the cold protects us
as we edge toward the middle of the month
toward some deadline that will render us impotent or worse

we do not discuss the situation
are separated from one another by the television
the w-word

the tension begins to build just after midnight
by morning we are rigid

January, the sixteenth

it comes as a betrayal
the moment the first bombs fall on Baghdad
I have been sitting inside the television all evening
the first prisoner of war
there is no escape

I have been preparing for this moment for weeks
bringing in additional supplies of coca cola and potato chips
I am not even sure when I might begin to look for a way out

January, after the sixteenth

quietly one night
I slip into the living room
turn on the television
yes, I am there, obviously
but growing restless, I am beginning to crawl around
make small noises

shortly before dawn I find a crack
between a bulletin and a commercial
no one is watching
no one asks for my passport
I slip out
casually

until someone seals the crack
I am able to come and go as I please

~

I am not alone
I share this wooden cell with others
pilots, prisoners of war
in such tight quarters I should be able to reach out
stroke their bruised faces

January, one afternoon

Risk, you buy the game with money you have saved
I will not buy it for you
you say it is a friendly game
explain the game to your friend
the pieces are armies, one side is black
one is red and there are other pieces, too, yellow ones
they change sides and the game depends on them, their
deployment
strategy and luck, that is the dangerous part, luck
that is why you play the game

you have played before
your friend is a novice, just learning about war
it takes time to explain the rules
when the game begins I am called
a neutral observer to be sure no pieces are moved
while you go to the bathroom
already you do not trust your friend
one of you stalls, the other protests
I set a deadline, the timer on the stove
I would prefer you went outside, curried 4-H calves
you insist the game must be finished, one of you must win
the squabbling continues, one of you strikes the other
I call time out, negotiations
both of you turn on me

on your way outside you tell your friend
        it was only a practice
        we'll play the real game some other day

January, the eighteenth

I am walking across the ranchyard when I hear bombers
loud, they will emerge from the blue clouds of winter
rumble over the farm
the fields resemble runways and I see cluster bombs
bouncing in the stubble

the yard is a major target
a missile is on its way
it will rip through fences
send the cattle bellering in all directions
render my collie helpless

the bombers are not bombers
it is the sound of a propane torch
thawing out a culvert blocked with ice
the missile is a contrail fading from sight

even a small aircraft overhead
suggests catastrophe

January, the twenty-seventh

I envy you, your stance
you do not let the war keep you
from all that must be done
the cattle that must be fed, the ice chopped
gates opened, closed again
dirty pigeons shitting on the rafters will be cursed
dogs praised
plastic twine burned,
tires repaired and filled with air again,
wheat augered from the bin into the truck
hauled to the elevator in town
you will have a coffee
gather the local news
and carry it home
I will know who had a new baby
who won last night's hockey game

you have already crawled out of your television set
I am still popping in and out of mine

January, the thirtieth

it is several hours since I last exposed myself
to television, the eye of war
I ask why I am writing these lines in the middle of the night
why I am not upstairs sleeping beside you

my sleep was disturbed by an owl, a sound so small
I am not sure whether it was a child dying
first death, or coming back to life

the last day of January

the war is already old
some say as old as Babylon, as old as sand
and dry river beds
only Methuselah knows

beyond the earth, satellites
new stars confuse old skies
old stargazers

beneath the northern lights
scud lines are crossing
and crisscrossing
creating some new display of incendiary imagination
I am unable to comprehend

sitting with Methuselah
I have given up television
I am locked on a very old star

call this place home

the morning when he tells her he must leave the ranch
tells her he can not do this – this rising at dawn
to check the heifers, a long day in the fields,
seeding, summerfallowing, swathing, baling, stacking, repairing
metal clanging against metal, humming in three octaves
home at noon   home again at dusk
the next day, the same or almost the same
his knees, his ankles swell like patched inner tubes

she layers a jacket over a vest over a sweater
once more to the pasture
she will count the cows she counted yesterday
check the same fences
open and shut the same gates
she could do it with her eyes closed

but she might miss the nighthawk on the corral fence
the goldenrod bursting in the west coulee
the water rippling over stones at the crossing

the crossing, she pauses
it has come to this, the crossing
the same creek they crossed forty-three years before

her heart, like his knees,
a patched inner tube

it is not as though she hasn't talked about this day
how she would move farther from town
live with a jar of matches, an axe, a woodpile
a place where wood must be chopped
where a wood stove flickers
        and ashes must be hauled out

where the water freezes in the creek
        and in a water pail
where frost swirls across window panes
and shingles splinter beneath stars

there she would sleep and wait
wait for spring
wait for a day
when cows with newborn calves come
to join her in the pasture
wait the way a coyote waits for afterbirth

it is not as though she hasn't talked about this
this turning back
her ashes

once more to the middle pasture

>   while sagehens strut in and out
>   amongst the sagebrush
>   while sharptails
>   lift from the grama grass
>   antelope circle around her

she whispers to the burrowing owls
tells them she will miss them
their arrivals and departures
>   all the days of sun and wind between
yes, she will miss them
>   their eyes sparkling in the morning light
>   their murmuring soft as dusk
she will miss them
and the scent of sage, of wolf willow
drifting toward her

she dreams of a cabin in the wilderness
a place to which there is no road
Yeats, her Irish brother, it is his poem
her dream

she did not know she wanted to trade
wattles and daub for poles and adobe
an island in a lake with water lapping on the shore
his Innisfree
        for the southwest corner of section twenty-six
a patch of prairie, all that is left of the original dream
a place where a solitary pipit might spiral from a cloud
and sing for its own amusement
the way she might hum the same lines of a song over and over
and yes, at noon, share a purple glow

she will borrow lines from his poem, lines remembered
the nine bean rows, something about bees
– no, scrap the bees
there are black flies in the goldenrod

she will arise and go now in search of his cabin – no
in search of her own

the ranch house becomes a bungalow
a patch of prairie traded for a garden plot
goldenrod for marigold
one creek for another

if only she could recall the words
      she could join Connie Kaldor in her praises
of the little Wood River
then she might call this place home

if only she could forget the Rock Creek waltz

they move, empty one room, the next
bedrooms become the same bedrooms in a different house
the living room, the same living room

    their son and his friends move the oak table
    the one her sister said she could keep for a lifetime
    the one old Caillier carved with his breadknife
    when it was still his table

    without leaves
    the table is large enough for a family of eight
    they should have had more children
    more reasons for staying

moving day, the same table
a different house

a granddaughter is disappointed –
all the same furniture, all the same paintings on the walls
all the same

they take the calico cat,
the one named Souffle, with them
     she was born by Caesarian section
she trembles when the door opens
trembles because one day she came back to the house
one day without a mother
trembles because she was covered in blood

in the new house the cat rubs against the furniture
the same familiar furniture
finds her place in his lap

the cat settles

the first six months she spills out of bed
so regular he could set the clock by the thump on the floor
her hip, black and bruised
the bedroom, a mirror image of the bedroom on the ranch
she is sleeping on the wrong side of the bed

awake in the night, she takes inventory
the pliers, the scissors
she has lost something
      where is the key to the safety deposit box?
top drawer, left-hand side
always in the same safe place
in the middle of the night she remembers
small drawers in the ranch house

she remembers what is lost

a year later she finds the baby pictures
their anniversary picture
upside down in the bottom of a cardboard box

she is still sleeping on the wrong side of the bed

sometimes in the night
she walks in her sleep
not dangerously just shuffling
one foot in front of the other
searching for the springhead, the tin cup
the water that will quench this long thirst
the sweet taste of moss and leaves

other nights she smacks her head on a wall
where there should be a door
she winces

some mornings, she sleeps late
there is no morning bird
no bird that wakes the other birds
no bird that wakes her

sometimes she wakes while it is still dark
watches as the stars fade
        the moon becomes invisible

a friend says if she hauls rocks from the ranch
creates a rock garden, the yard will claim her
she gathers sandstone, petrified wood and feldspar
plants them in the garden
with creeping cedar, crocuses, beardtongue

from poplar tree to poplar tree
a blight moves along the boulevard
moves into the rock garden
one by one the plants die
their leaves, like letters edged in black

she must learn to garden all over again
the rocks are the only living things in her garden

twice she tries to transplant a bearberry

once, by herself
she finds a clump of bearberry in a patch of red
lilies blooming on a slumped hillside
she leaves the lilies
plies the woody roots of the bearberry
spades away the clay
reaches into the darkness
knots the roots and lifts the plant from the earth
hauls it home and buries the roots in her front yard

three days later the leaves crumble in her hands
the branches become sticks

next, with a granddaughter
she finds the plant in an upland ditch
the woody roots just as stubborn
just as rooted as before
together they twist the plant from the earth
move it to the rock garden

again, the leaves crumble
she knows the branches will soon be sticks

knows some plants grow best where they are rooted

this place so dry, the grass dies before it blossoms
the crocus sleeps

mornings begin with the same red glow
the red shadow of the last sunset

have you ever seen the colour of dust?

the only sound, tinder in the grass
her heart breaking

the colour of spring, summer, autumn
the colour dry

she lives on the other side of the hills

her last quarter of land is transferred
how easy it was to sign the agreement of sale
sign away the last prairie
the place where coyotes run
raise their young –
once she could hold them in her eyes
yellow pups beside a mound of yellow clay
the camouflage of sun and shadows
wind playing with pups

and what of the meadowlarks
braced against the wind
questioning and answering

will the prairie sing the way it did before
will it still be prairie?

wanting to be near him
more than near anyone else
she crowds the bed
pushes against him

he sleeps with one arm
braced against the floor
holding his body
on the edge of the bed

the last day of winter
becomes the first day of spring
she leaves the premises
goes wandering
searches for pussy willows
moss phlox
she is drawn farther and farther

while he sleeps
she searches for flowers

one evening he brings flowers
creamy roses tied with a pink ribbon

before they wilt
she hangs them on the wall upside down
a reminder of other roses
how he drove all the way home from the far side of the pasture
opened and shut five gates
to take her all the way back, show her a patch of pink
roses embroidered on the banks of Hellfire

he brings roses
roses so she can recall the scent of roses
the scent of pink

at night the animals come
three deer say, *follow us*
she sees thin shadows on the grass
the deer luminescent

another night, a bush rabbit
hunches by the cherry tree
blinks and waits for her to come out
follow its tracks

a lone moose takes a turn
tracks a perfect circle in the snow
once, twice around the ash tree
she hears it snuffle, *come, come*

all around the village
coyotes howl
they want her too

forty-three years on the ranch
she counts the birds in the yard
marks their arrival in the bird book
the slate coloured junco, myrtle warblers, a pair of shrikes
a bobolink, the first she has ever seen, then another
two ruby crowned kinglets
six robins, and a kingbird

she notes when chaos erupts in the upper branches
the jostling for nests
notes the brown thrasher, how he settles the quarrels
     how the nesting begins again

early autumn,
when she moves north to this village
birds are left behind
that same autumn seven geese fly over the village
she wills her spirit fly south with them
     her flight denied

late winter she waits
waits for birds and birdsong
what she misses most is
birds

March, nine Hungarian partridges
lead three alley cats through powdery snow
a little faster, a little faster
click, click

April, she glimpses a scrap of orange
lighting the maple trees in the neighbor's yard
hears notes of a song she has never heard before
sees a bird she has never seen

and on the west side of the village
two peregrine falcons stake their claim
one shuffles on a nest
the other struts on the ridge cap of a grain elevator
plunges, feet first
prepared to pluck the gold from her granddaughter's hair

this very winter, last week or the week before
she hears an owl huff
as it swoops from yard to yard
some say there are two owls, some say three

neighbours claim the birds
the falcons belong to a bachelor
a widow names the oriole
two boys speak the language of owls
the partridges leave town

August, a blue heron
lifts from a barren platform
high in verdant poplars at the head of Rock Creek
hunches into its wings and crosses the divide
follows the creek into the village
flaps and glides, flaps and glides so slowly
so slowly over the creek
snaking behind her house
it is her heron

birds come slowly

soon, she will join a band of birdwatchers
binoculars in hand she will ascend the bench
roam the hills between the headwaters of Rock Creek
and Wood River

she will scout the ridges
find places where the earth rolls over itself
slumps where updrafts carry small birds
high above the horizon
where a single bird rises
where a single note echoes
    a bent note
        dropped into a tin pail
  into a new summer

Acknowledgements

Some of these poems have previously appeared in the following magazines: Fiddlehead, Grain, Pierian Spring, Maverick Verse, Prairie Fire, and Premium Swift Review. Others were first printed in anthologies: *Heading Out* (Coteau Books) *Cowboy Poetry Matters* (Story Line Press), *A Labour of Love* (Polestar), *Woven on the Wind* (Houghton Mifflin), and *Maverick Verse* (Gibbs Smith).

New Orleans, Saskatchewan was performed at Globe Theatre and aired on CBC Radio. Also on the CBC were *the last peregrine* and some of the poems from the January file.

Special thanks to my editor Bob Currie for his insights and useful criticism. Many thanks to Geoffrey Ursell and Barbara Sapergia who followed a lot of the small steps along the way and never gave up on the manuscript.

Thanks also to Nellie Spicer for her generous comments and to Doris Bircham, Anne Slade, Sharon Butala and Karen Farge for their continuing encouragement. I would be amiss not to mention some of those who have hiked the hills along Rock Creek with me at one time or another, in particular Colleen Raes and Sandra Knoss. Others who have inspired me will recognize themselves in the poetry.

About the Author

Thelma Poirier is the author of three previous Coteau
Books publications – the memoir *Rock Creek* and the poetry
collections *Grasslands, the Private Hearings* and *Double Visions*.
She has written two books for young readers, *Children of the
Wood Mountain Uplands* and *The Bead Pot*, as well as portions
of the *Field Guide to the Grasslands National Park*.

Thelma has had a hand in editing five books on the
ranching life: *Beyond the Range, Cowgirls: 100 Years of Writing
the Range, Grass Roots, Wood Mountain Uplands* and *A Voice of
Her Own*.

Thelma Poirier spent most of her youth and adult life on
ranches near Fir Mountain, Saskatchewan, moving to the
nearby village of Glentworth in 2003. Ranching, the natural
environment and history remain her special interests.